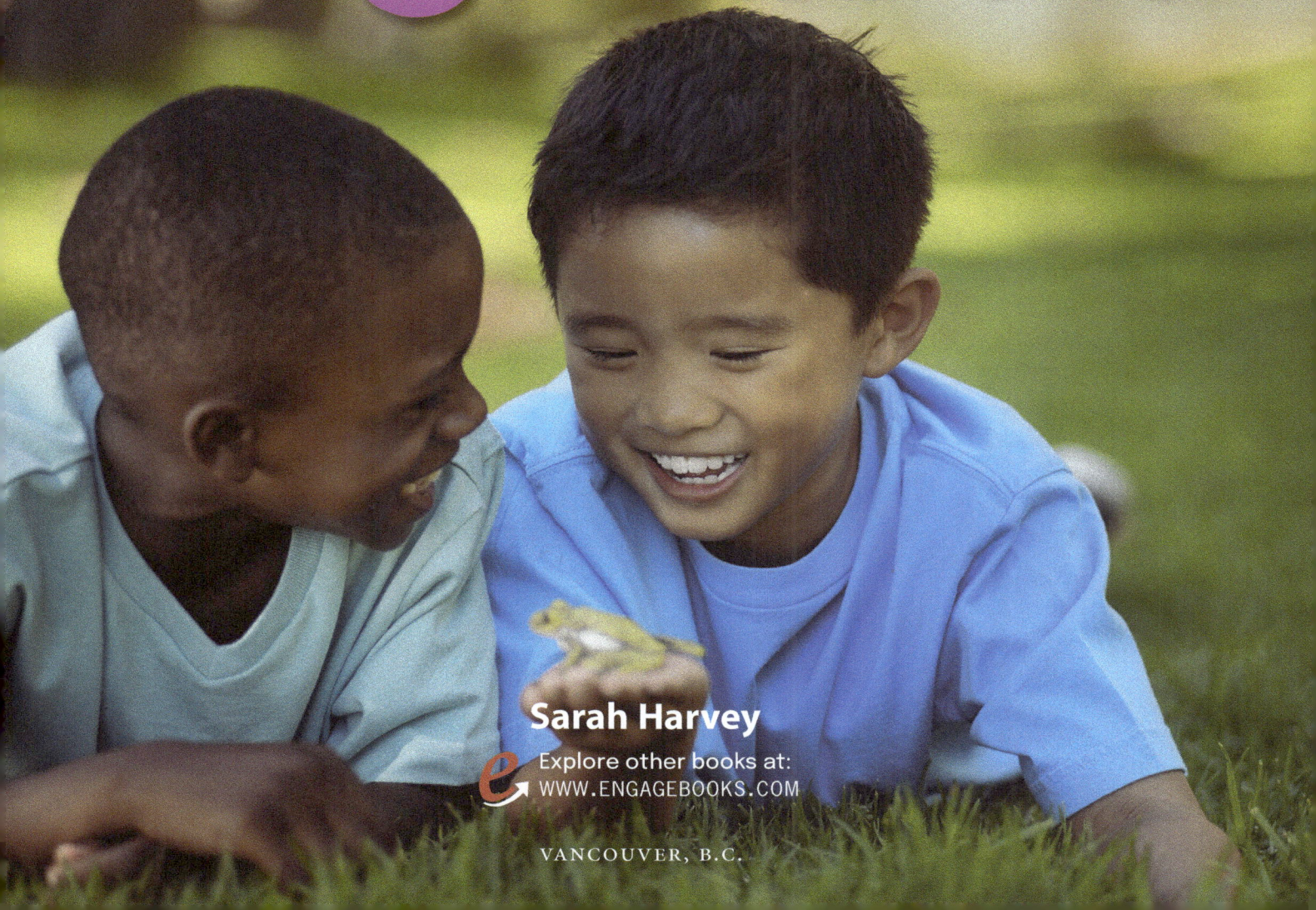

Animals &ME

Frogs and Me

Sarah Harvey

Explore other books at:
WWW.ENGAGEBOOKS.COM

VANCOUVER, B.C.

e → WWW.ENGAGEBOOKS.COM

Frogs and Me
Animals and Me
Edited by: A.R. Roumanis
Text © 2022 Engage Books
Design © 2022 Engage Books

Text set in GelPenUpright

FIRST EDITION / FIRST PRINTING

LIBRARY AND ARCHIVES CANADA CATALOGUING IN PUBLICATION

Title: Frogs and me / by Sarah Harvey.
Names: Harvey, Sarah N., 1950- author.
Description: Series statement: Animals and me

Identifiers: Canadiana (print) 20220395446 | Canadiana (ebook) 20220395454
ISBN 978-1-77476-696-5 (hardcover)
ISBN 978-1-77476-697-2 (softcover)
ISBN 978-1-77476-698-9 (epub)
ISBN 978-1-77476-699-6 (pdf)

Subjects:
LCSH: Frogs—Juvenile literature.
LCSH: Frogs—Behavior—Juvenile literature.
LCSH: Human behavior—Juvenile literature.

Classification: LCC QL668.E2 H37 2022 | DDC J597.8/9—DC23

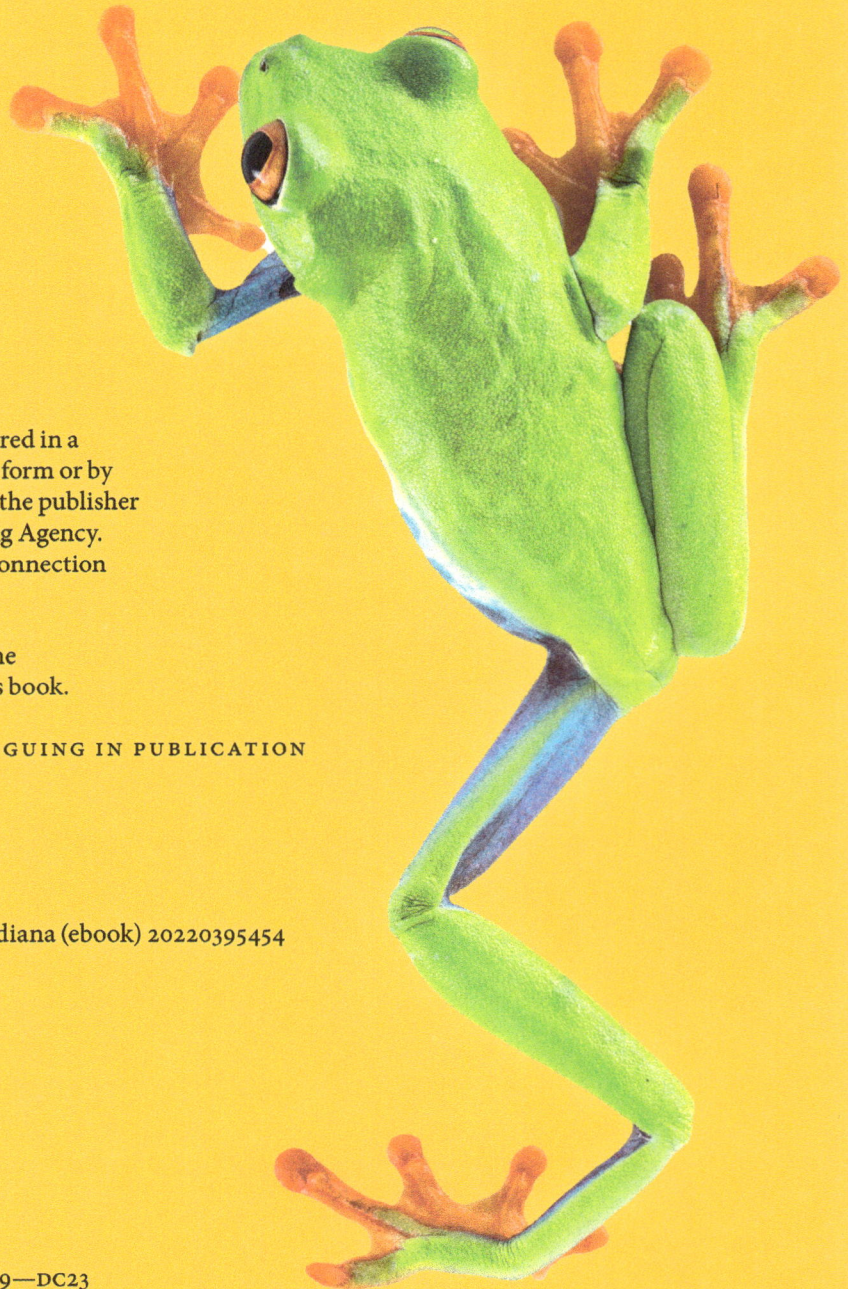

This project has been made possible in part by the Government of Canada.

Canada

Have you ever seen a frog?

3

Frogs need to live
near water.

4

Do you live near the water?

Baby frogs are called tadpoles.

They look like tiny fish.

What did you look like
when you were born?

7

Some frogs sleep in trees.
Some sleep in water.
And some sleep underground.

What's the strangest place you've ever slept?

Frogs use their long, sticky tongues to catch and eat insects.

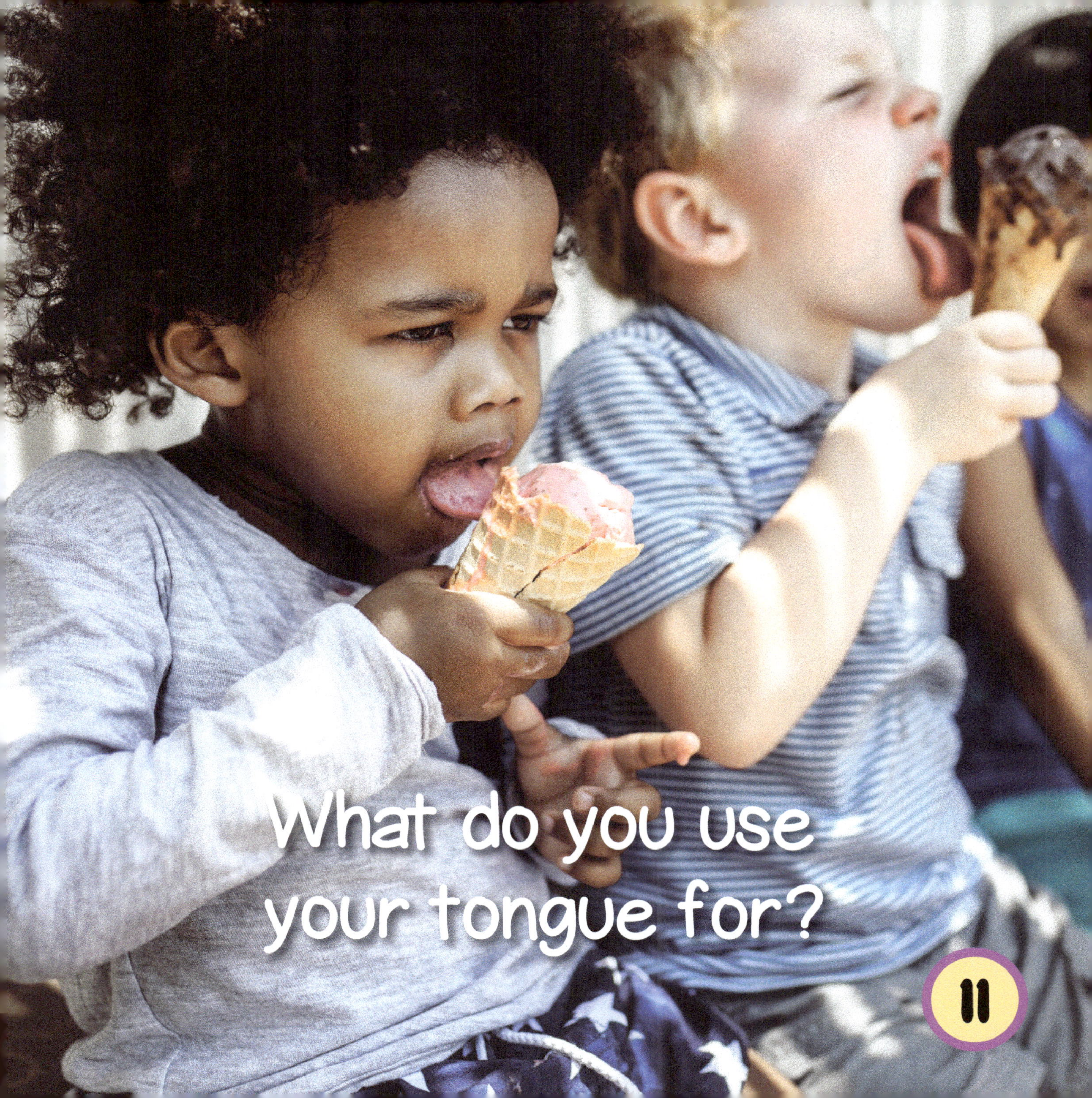

What do you use your tongue for?

Frogs talk to each other by croaking and chirping.

What other animal chirps?

Male frogs have a big pouch so they can croak really loudly.

What's the loudest animal sound you can make?

Frogs are fantastic jumpers because of their long back legs.

Have you ever played leapfrog?

Frogs can see really well at night.

WHOO else has great night vision?

19

Goliath frogs are the biggest frogs in the world. They can weigh up to 7 pounds (3 kilograms).

Do you know something else that weighs about 7 pounds (3 kg)?

The smallest frog in the world is the size of a housefly. They are very hard to find.

What's the tiniest animal you have ever seen?

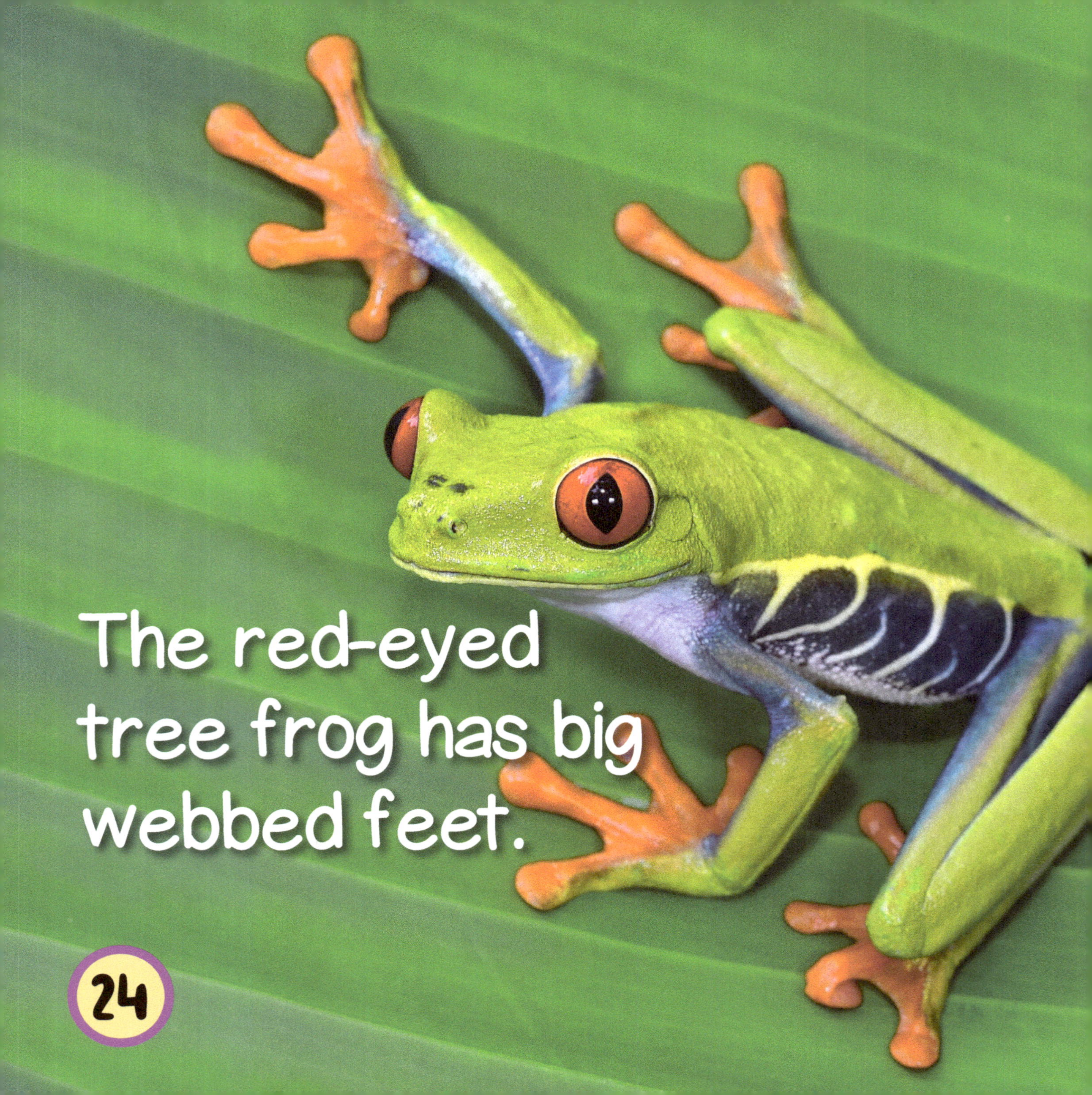

The red-eyed tree frog has big webbed feet.

What other animal
has webbed feet?

25

The tomato frog is the same color as a ripe tomato.

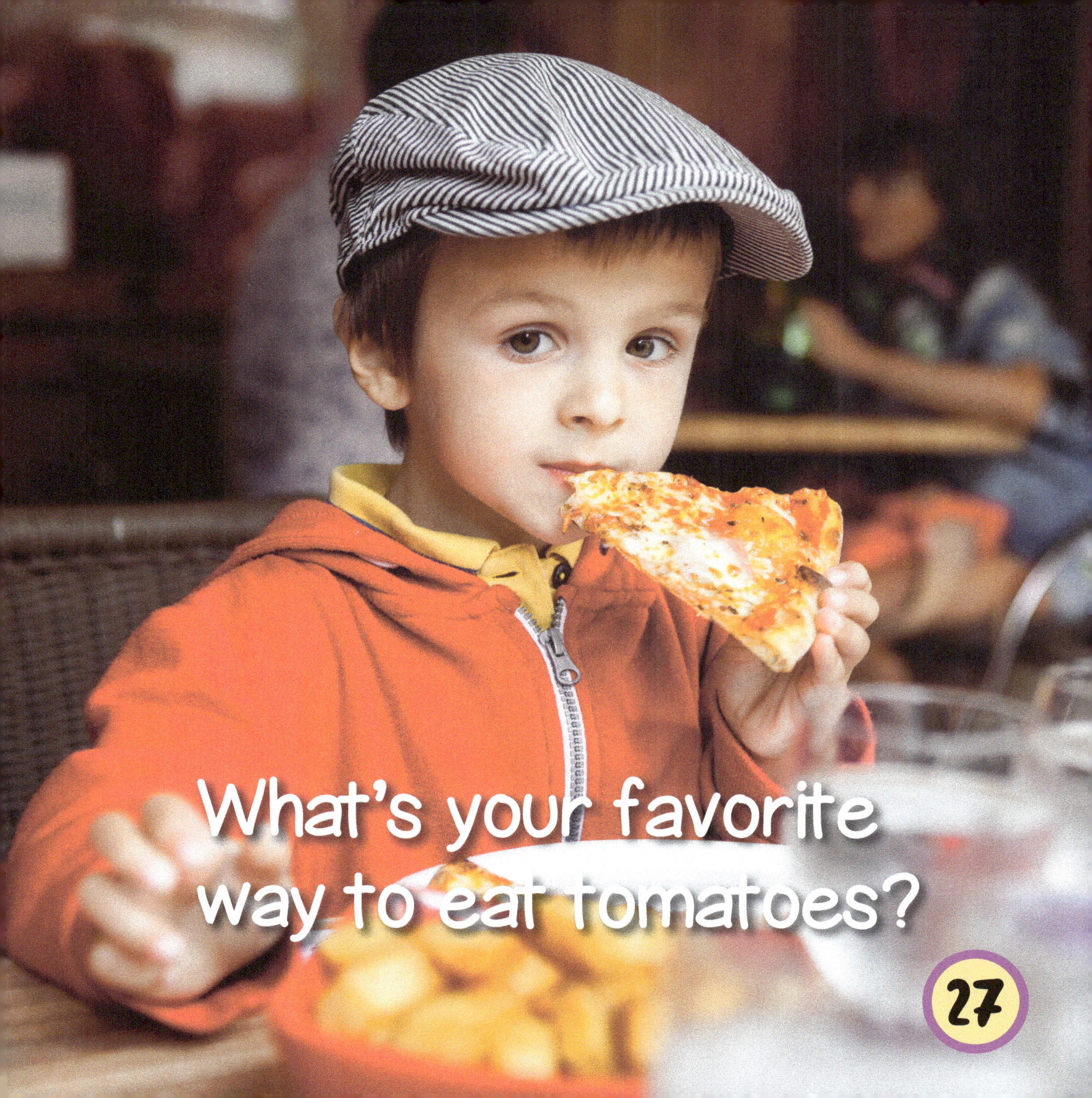

What's your favorite way to eat tomatoes?

The desert rain frog likes to burrow in the sand.

Do you like to play in the sand?

Sometimes frogs like
to hang out together.

Who do you like to
hang out with?

www.ingramcontent.com/pod-product-compliance
Lightning Source LLC
Chambersburg PA
CBHW041435040426
42452CB00023B/2982